Blood & Gore

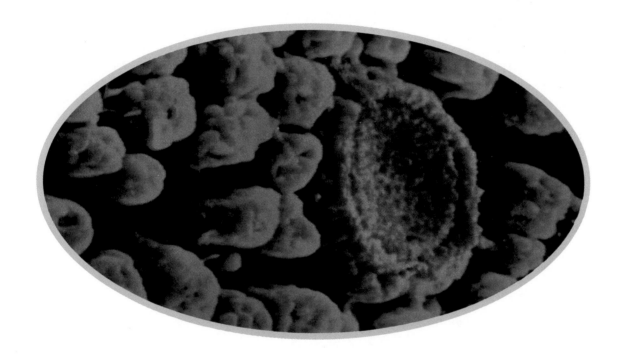

LIKE YOU'VE NEVER SEEN!

Vicki Cobb

Scholastic Inc.

New York   Toronto   London   Auckland   Sydney

For Judy Jensen Cobb

Photo Credits

Magnifications of the images are in parenthesis following the page number.

Cover: Dennis Kunkel, Kailua, Hawaii/Phototake: front (x2,317,612), back top left (x639,450), back center (x229,425); Omikron/SPL/Photo Researchers: back top right (x26,649); G. T. Hewlett/Narcotics Education, Inc.: back bottom left; Moredun Animal Health Ltd./SPL/Photo Researchers: back bottom right (x2,268,000).

Interior: Peter Arnold: 3 (x168,000), 8 (x126,000); Chris Bjornberg/SPL/Photo Researchers: 15 right (enhanced X ray); Dee Breger: 5 bottom (x4,357,500), 19 (x3500 as reproduced); CNRI/SPL/Photo Researchers: 17 (x982,800), 20 (x458,325), 26 (x1,461,600); Nancy Eckman, p. 32 bottom; G. T. Hewlett/Narcotics Education, Inc.: 30, 31; Dennis Kunkel, Kailua, Hawaii/Phototake: 4 left (x9,442,125), 4 right (x894,600), 5 top (x598,500), 6-7 (x2,124,150), 10 left (x649,687), 11 (x404,250), 16 left (x57,750), 16 right (x78,750), 18 (x1,290,712), 21 (x593,775), 22 (x42,000), 23 (x7350), 24 (x34,650), 32 top (x758,625), 32 middle (x379,312); Moredun Animal Health Ltd./SPL/Photo Researchers: 29 (x4,762,800); Professor P. Motta, Department of Anatomy, University *La Sapienza,* Rome/SPL/Photo Researchers: 13 left (x24,675), 13 right (x756,000), 14-15 (x7,392,000), 27 inset (x24,255), 27 background (x46,200), 28 (x17,272); Omikron/SPL/Photo Researchers: 1 (x90,804), 25 (x64,155); Andrew Syred/SPL/Photo Researchers: 9 (x38,220), 10 right (x248,062), 12 (x330,750).

BOOK DESIGN BY KEVIN CALLAHAN/BNGO BOOKS

Library of Congress Cataloging-in-Publication Data

Cobb, Vicki
Blood and gore, like you've never seen/ / by Vicki Cobb.
p. cm.
Includes index.
ISBN 0-590-92665-9
1. Cytology—Atlases—Juvenile literature. 2. Scanning electron microscopy—Atlases—Juvenile literature. I Title.

QH582.5.C63	1997
611.o81—dc21	96-37971
	CIP
	AC

1 2 3 4 5 6 7 8 9 10   62   13 12 11 10 09 08 07 06

Printed in China
First Scholastic printing, September 1997

Contents

Blood

Ouch! Blood! Not a happy sight! A little blood is not serious. A lot of blood can mean death. Since ancient times people have known that blood is the red liquid that comes out of wounded people and animals. Blood and life are connected. But how? Some of blood's secrets are revealed by extraordinary pictures taken with a very modern invention—the electron microscope. It magnifies things hundreds, even many thousands, of times larger than their actual size.

Oxygen, Coming Right Up

A drop of blood the size of the dot at the end of a sentence is packed with five million red blood cells. Each tiny red cell looks like a doughnut with a dent instead of a hole. Red cells are like tiny rafts floating through your body in a river of about five quarts of a straw-colored liquid called *plasma.*

Why red? The red pigment, called *hemoglobin,* contains iron. When iron combines with oxygen it turns red. So the job of hemoglobin is to combine with oxygen. Red cells pick up oxygen in the lungs. The heart pumps them through sixty thousand miles of arteries, veins, and capillaries on a round-trip journey. They deliver the life-giving oxygen to every other cell in the body. They pick up carbon dioxide, a waste gas, and return to the lungs for us to breathe it out. The red cells are now ready for another load of oxygen.

The shape of red cells gives them a larger surface area for exchanging oxygen and carbon dioxide

gases. It also makes them very flexible. Red cells are often bent and squeezed as they are pushed through the tiny capillaries.

Enemies, Beware!

No, this is not a weapon from outer space. But it *is* a weapon. Fortunately, it's one that fights on your side. This is a kind of white blood cell, called a **macrophage,** attacking some purple germs. The macrophage extends threadlike arms to capture the tiny bacteria surrounding it. A captured germ is then drawn back inside the macrophage, where it is digested. There is one white cell for every thousand red cells—a huge army ready to fight a war. "Eating" the enemy is just one of several clever ways different types of white cells protect us from disease.

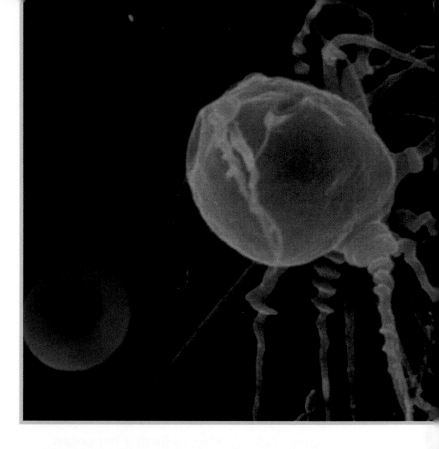

Picking Up the Trash

This "walking" macrophage is caught in the act of cleaning a tiny air space in a lung sick with pneumonia. White cells die after "eating" their fill of pneumonia germs. The dead cell bodies are removed by other white cells. This garbage-removing macrophage extends a long tube, almost like a vacuum cleaner hose. Macrophages move by changing shape and squeezing themselves through spaces between other cells. There is no place in your body that they cannot go.

5

Stop the Flood!

A cut is an emergency. Your blood instantly responds to stop itself from pouring out of you. Chemicals released by injured cells set off a chain of events. The end result is the formation of a blood clot anywhere, anytime blood is leaking where it shouldn't.

There are two parts to the blood-clotting system. One part is made of protein molecules called **fibrinogen** and is dissolved in the blood plasma. Fibrinogen can be changed into tiny solid **fibrin threads**—the heart of a clot—but only when there is a trigger. This trigger is made of other chemicals inside the fifteen million tiniest free-floating cell pieces, called **platelets,** found in every drop of blood.

When you are injured, damaged tissues give off substances that start a chain of events. The platelets immediately stick together to form a temporary plug. Then they release a chemical that triggers the formation of the fibrin. Within two minutes of the injury, the fibrin threads trap red and white blood cells to make a clot. In this picture, red cells are red, platelets are blue, and fibrin threads are yellow.

When the clot first forms, the fibrin threads are stretched out. Then they tighten, squeezing out a clear fluid called blood **serum.** Serum is plasma without the ability to clot. The entire construction dries out and toughens, forming a scab. Under the scab, the wound heals as damaged skin and muscle cells replace themselves. Good job!

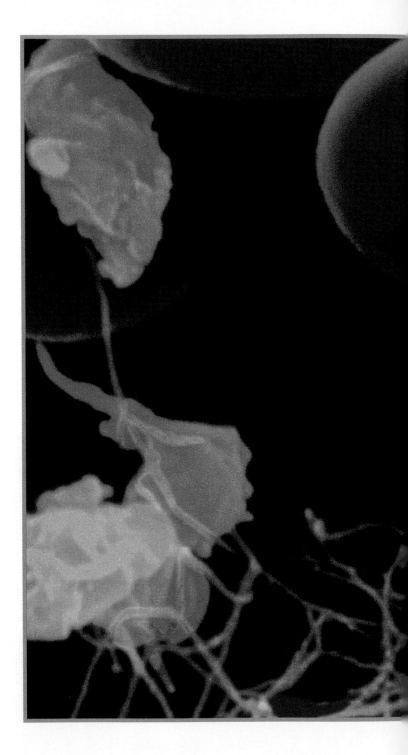

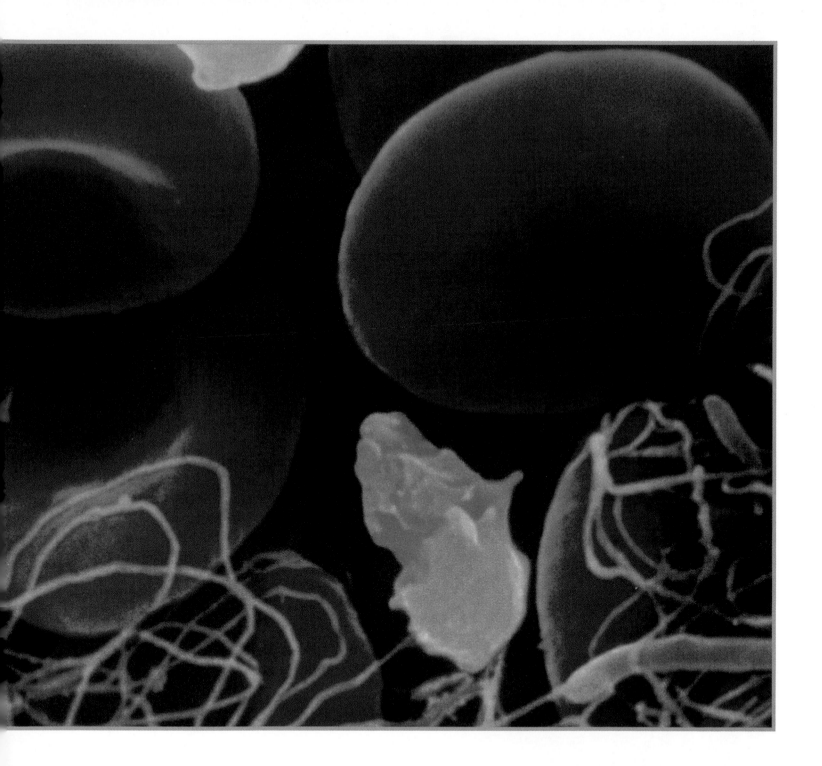

Skin

● ● ● ● ● ● ●

Blood and gore are hidden as long as your skin is not broken. Your amazing skin keeps your insides inside you and the dangers of the outside from getting in. When you are wounded, it repairs itself. Why isn't it tougher? If it were as tough as a suit of armor, you'd have a hard time moving.

Skin is a truly amazing organ, the largest one in your body. When you're grown, your skin can cover two square yards and weigh more than nine pounds. It is considered an organ because it does so many specialized jobs in addition to protecting your insides. When you sweat, your skin helps cool you off. When it's cold, your skin puckers into goose bumps and sends blood deeper in the body, where it's warmer. And of course, skin is where your sense of touch is located.

Pavement from Your Cheek

These skin cells were scraped from the inside of a cheek, stained, and then photographed through an ordinary light microscope. You can see the cell nucleus in the center surrounded by the cell's living material—its *cytoplasm*. The skin inside your cheek can be more delicate and thinner than your outside skin because it is constantly bathed in mucus and saliva, which protect it. These flat cells fit together like paving stones when they're in your mouth and there are layers of them. The top layer is constantly being shed, so scraping the cheek did not injure the person who provided these cells. In fact, you shed almost a million dead skin cells from all over your body each hour of the day! But don't worry, your skin is always growing new cells to replace them. You produce so many that every month you have a completely new skin.

8

A Five o'clock Shadow

No, this is not some kind of weird forest. This picture is called a scanning electron micrograph, or **SEM** for short. It is skin from a man's face sprouting his not-so-newly shaved beard. The skin's surface is made up of twenty-five layers of dead cells. Skin cells die as **keratin** forms inside them. Keratin is a tough protein that does not dissolve in water and is indigestible.

Hair is made up of another kind of keratin with scales that overlap like the shingles on a roof. The root of each hair is enclosed in a cuplike pocket of skin called the **hair follicle.** The hair looks like a log because it grows outward from a central core like a tree. Every once in a while a hair follicle withers and the hair falls out. Then it rests for three or four months before growing a new hair. You lose about thirty to sixty hairs a day.

Hair is the fastest-growing part of the body. Head hair grows almost five inches a year. A single follicle can produce twenty-six feet of hair in a lifetime. A man's beard grows an inch every three months. In some men, that's enough to be a noticeable beard shadow after eight hours. Get the razor!

Tough Stuff

The job of an eyelash is to protect the eye from dust. Eyelashes are considered beautiful. This SEM shows an eyelash that has been coated with mascara to make it look thicker. You can also see that the goopy mascara acts as glue for an occasional shed skin cell.

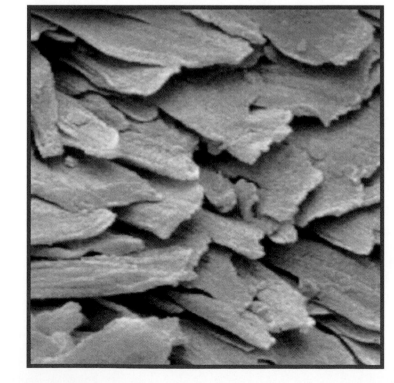

The SEM below is of a fingernail. The flattened structures are formed from dead skin cells at the nailbed at the base of a nail. They are almost pure keratin. They are linked together with a kind of keratin glue to form a tough protective layer. It takes about six months for a nail to grow from the nailbed to the tip of the finger. But fingernails don't all grow at the same rate. The longer the finger, the faster the nail grows. So your middle fingernail wins the race.

Death from a Day in the Sun

Yes, this is a wasteland. It's an SEM of the very dead skin of a sunburn. The hair has broken off and no longer grows above the hair follicle, which looks like an empty crater. One of the skin's jobs is to protect you from the sun. Sometimes it has to sacrifice itself to do so. Make no mistake: A sunburn is a burn, and a burn injury kills cells.

A history of sunburns can cause skin cancer many years later. In spite of this, many people want to expose their skin to the sun to get tan. Tanning develops a dark pigment in the skin cells, called **melanin,** which protects the skin from harmful rays. People who originally came from countries near the equator, where the sun's rays shine very directly, have naturally darker skin. Everyone should avoid long periods in the sun and use sunblock to protect their skin.

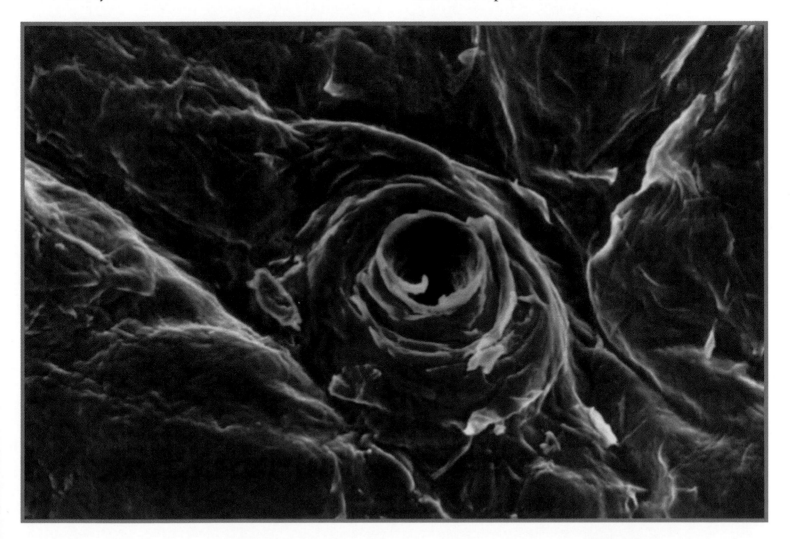

Bone

You would be a blob without your bones. The 206 bones of your skeleton support the weight of your body, giving it its basic shape and allowing it to move in countless ways. The word "skeleton" comes from a Greek word meaning "dried up." Obviously the Greeks were thinking about bones from a graveyard. But living bones are very different—one-fifth of their weight is water. They are also amazingly strong. The key to the way they do their job is in the way they're built.

Living Reinforced Concrete

The thigh bone, or *femur,* is the longest bone in your body, running between your hip and your knee. Its strength is partly due to its shape, which is more or less like a cylinder. (Rolled-up newspaper is a lot stronger than a flat sheet.) The outer layer of the bone is very dense. This SEM is looking down on a bone that has been sliced across its length. In the center is a tubelike *Haversian canal* containing blood vessels and nerves. Haversian canals run parallel to the length of a bone and interconnect with each other. This way they can deliver nourishment to the bone cells called *osteoblasts.* Layers of bone, which you see as rings surrounding the Haversian canal, are formed by the osteoblasts, which live in the small dark areas.

Dense Bone

Concrete reinforced with steel rods has the strength of concrete and the flexibility of steel. Your bones have a similar structure. This SEM is a closer look at the outside surface of a bone. It shows the sheetlike layers of bone laid down by the osteoblasts. There are fibers in the layers that are made of flexible protein. The fibers are stuck together and strengthened with minerals—mostly calcium, which makes them hard and dense. Almost half of the weight of your bones is due to its minerals that you get from dairy food.

Spongy Bone

The core of the femur and other large bones is made up of an open honeycomb of spongy or *cancellous bone.* This SEM shows the cavities formed by columns and bridges of cancellous bone. If the femur were solid, it would be too heavy to move easily. Cancellous bone keeps it lightweight. In a living bone, these cavities are filled with bone marrow, which produces both red and white blood cells in enormous quantities. Every second your bone marrow makes two million new red blood cells.

Human Plastic

Your joints and your spine are places where bones could crunch against bones because they are so close. Your nose and ears stick out from your head and are easily hit. Your body needs a smooth, tough, flexible material to serve as a cushion. *Cartilage* is your body's version of a tough plastic. It is found at the ends of long bones—such as the hip, shoulder, knee, and elbow—and as disks between the bones of your spine and at the tip of your nose and your outer ears.

This picture is an SEM of the cartilage that covers the end of the femur at your knee. On the bottom are the rounded shapes of a flexible white

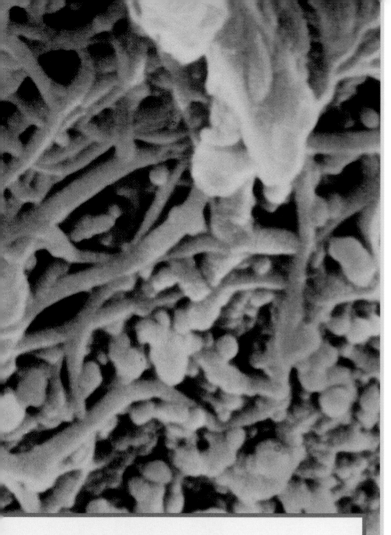

protein called *collagen.* On the top are the yellowish fibers of a protein called *elastin.* Collagen fills in the spaces between the elastin fibers, creating a flexible and extremely smooth material. It makes sure that the knee joint moves easily over a lifetime of stepping, standing, sitting, and doing deep knee bends.

Uh-oh

This is a computer-colored X ray of—you guessed it—a broken bone. When this skier's foot came to a sudden stop, his body kept going forward. The front leg bone, the tibia, snapped against the top of the ski boot. Fortunately, bones can heal themselves. New bone grows from each part of the break toward the other. It takes four to six months for an adult broken bone to heal completely. A child's broken bone heals five times faster.

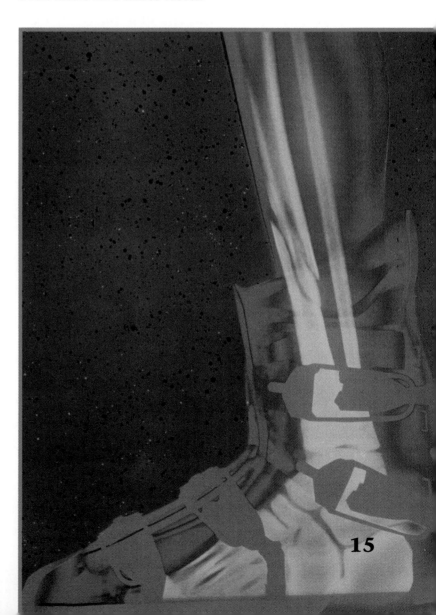

15

Muscle

● ● ● ● ● ● ●

Meat is muscle. The muscle in your body looks very much like the steaks and chops you see in the grocery store. Your muscles make up the largest organ in your body by weight. In a one-hundred-pound child, forty-two pounds are muscle.

The job of muscle is to move your skeleton. You have 620 skeletal muscles working in pairs. Tendons attach each end of a muscle to a bone. When your biceps (on the front of your upper arm) contracts, your lower arm moves up. When its partner, your triceps (on the back of your upper arm), contracts, your lower arm moves down. When it contracts, a muscle gets thicker in the middle and shorter. Feel the bulge in the middle of your biceps when you contract it. The stronger you are, the bigger the bulge and the harder the muscle.

Scientists use the light microscope and the electron microscope to help discover just how muscles contract.

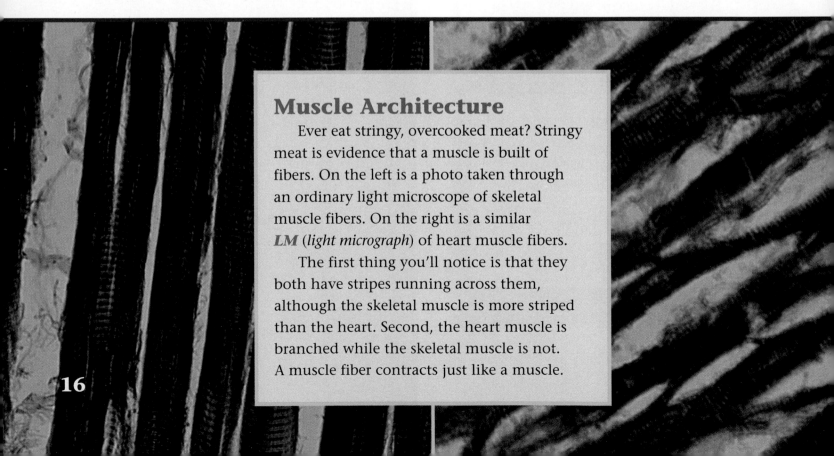

Muscle Architecture

Ever eat stringy, overcooked meat? Stringy meat is evidence that a muscle is built of fibers. On the left is a photo taken through an ordinary light microscope of skeletal muscle fibers. On the right is a similar *LM* (*light micrograph*) of heart muscle fibers.

The first thing you'll notice is that they both have stripes running across them, although the skeletal muscle is more striped than the heart. Second, the heart muscle is branched while the skeletal muscle is not. A muscle fiber contracts just like a muscle.

Living Springs

The scanning electron microscope lets us zoom in for a closer look. This SEM shows that a muscle fiber is made up of bundles of even smaller fibers, some of which are missing at the top. The stripes, called *striations,* show up as ridges across the length of the fibers. Two different proteins form the striations. During a contraction, the proteins slide past each other. One grips the other as if it were climbing a ladder. The striations are then closer together and the muscle is shorter. When the muscle relaxes, the proteins slide back to their original positions. Muscles contract in only one direction. That's why they must work in pairs.

Microscopic Power Plants

The muscle striations in this electron micrograph are the red and yellow bands. The big blob in the middle is a muscle cell nucleus. The purple blobs, called **mitochondria,** are the secret to the energy you need to move your muscles. Make no mistake: Moving takes energy!

The mighty mitochondria are like tiny power plants. They use oxygen and sugar to produce tiny packets of energy that power the contraction of the muscle proteins. Mitochondria are sprinkled throughout all the cells of your body. But muscle cells have an especially large number of them since they use so much energy.

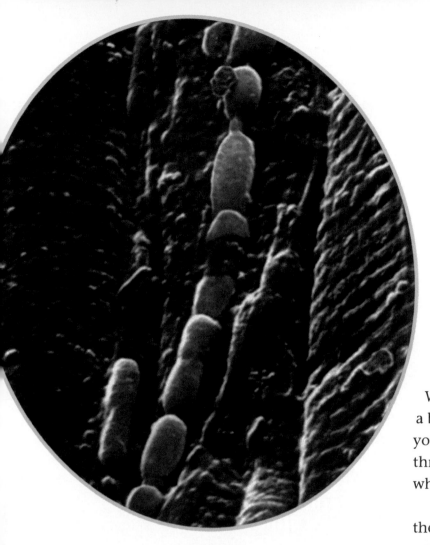

withstand that kind of workout. This SEM shows an up-close view of heart muscle fibers, with some capillaries, the smallest of blood vessels, running along the surface.

As you might expect, a workhorse muscle must have its own source of nourishing, oxygen-rich blood. It can't afford to run out of oxygen. When skeletal muscle runs out of oxygen, you get a burning sensation. But this doesn't happen to your heart muscle. This supermuscle uses more than three-fourths of the oxygen supplied by the blood while the skeletal muscles only use one-fourth.

The capillaries in this SEM look lumpy because they are collapsed due to low blood pressure. There are probably only a few red cells trapped in each sausage-shaped section. Blood pressure is strongest immediately after blood leaves the heart on its way through the body. It is strong enough to shoot a column of blood six feet into the air. This is enough to make sure that even the tiniest capillaries can deliver their life-giving fluid to cells in the body. Low blood pressure means that some cells—including some heart cells—aren't going to get their full share.

The Heart of the Heart

The job of your heart is to pump your blood through the ninety thousand miles of blood vessels in your body, making a thousand complete circuits a day. This amazing organ pumps two ounces of blood with every beat—that's about a gallon a minute—and when you exercise, it can pump twice as much. Only an extraordinary muscle can

Nerves

● ● ● ● ● ● ●

The inside world of your body communicates with itself and with the outside world through your nervous system. From the top of your head to the tips of your toes you are wired with a network of nerves. These living cables are constantly transmitting messages to keep your body running smoothly. You are unaware of most of these messages—those that keep your heart, intestines, liver, and lungs doing their jobs. But the nerves that get information from your senses and the ones that move your muscles are essential for the way you experience the world.

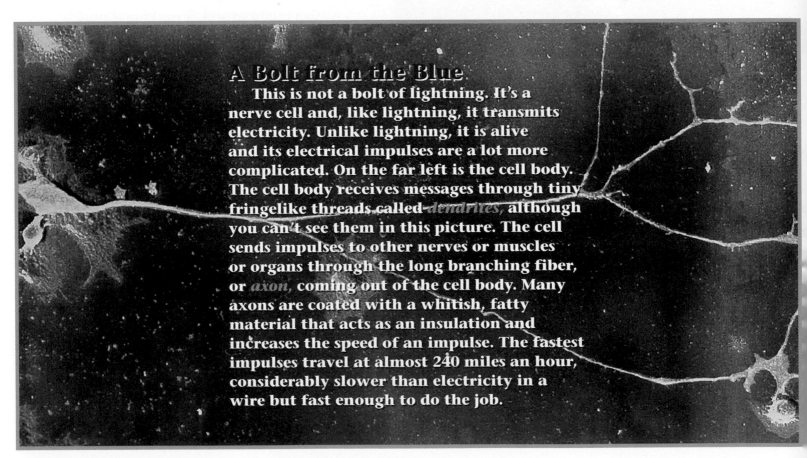

A Bolt from the Blue

This is not a bolt of lightning. It's a nerve cell and, like lightning, it transmits electricity. Unlike lightning, it is alive and its electrical impulses are a lot more complicated. On the far left is the cell body. The cell body receives messages through tiny fringelike threads called *dendrites*, although you can't see them in this picture. The cell sends impulses to other nerves or muscles or organs through the long branching fiber, or *axon*, coming out of the cell body. Many axons are coated with a whitish, fatty material that acts as an insulation and increases the speed of an impulse. The fastest impulses travel at almost 240 miles an hour, considerably slower than electricity in a wire but fast enough to do the job.

Care and Feeding

Nerve cells are one of the most highly specialized cells in the body. Like royalty, they are not bothered with the ordinary tasks of daily living. They are greatly outnumbered by a staff of servant cells that support them and protect them.

The nerve cell in this SEM looks something like a fried egg with three orange dendrites coming out of it. The thin yellow fiber is an axon. It is extended over a multifibered *astrocyte glial cell*, named for its starlike appearance. Among other jobs, glial cells are in charge of the care and feeding of nerves. A glial cell is like a multilegged octopus—each fiber can extend between and around nerve cells to nourish them. Astrocytes are found in the brain and spinal cord. Astrocytes have a whitish appearance. They make up the so-called "white matter" of the brain. When the brain or spinal cord is damaged, astrocytes are responsible for forming a scar that prevents nerve cells from regenerating. That's why a spinal cord injury has always meant permanent paralysis. New research, however, shows that it's possible to trick the glial cells so that the nerves can repair themselves. Perhaps, soon, paralyzed people will again be able to walk.

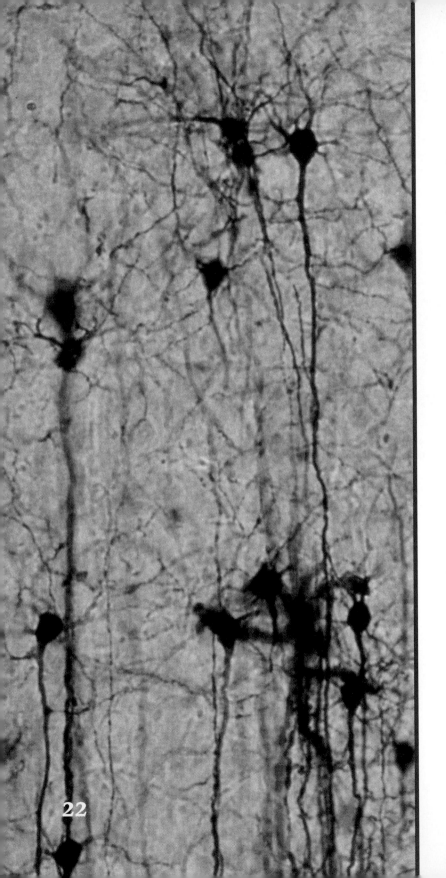

The Human Computer

This micrograph shows the "thinking" part of the brain—the *cerebrum*. The cerebrum is the outer layer of your brain just under your skull. This is an old-fashioned light microscope view that gave scientists their first look at just how complicated the brain is. This slide was prepared in the manner invented by Camillo Golgi, a nineteenth-century Italian scientist. First, a piece of brain tissue was treated chemically to preserve the cells. Next, it was treated with a type of silver. The fine structures of some of the nerves attract the silver and show up as black lines and blobs. Finally the tissue was sliced thin enough for light to pass through it before mounting it on a glass slide. Golgi's stain showed that nerves are not continuous but that there are distinct but very tiny gaps between nerve cells.

The nerves in this micrograph are called *pyramidal cells*, because the cell body has a triangular shape, like a pyramid. They are found in the part of the cerebrum that controls the movements your body makes.

The Programmer

This is an enlargement of a ten times magnification of a Golgi stained slice of the *cerebellum*—a part of the brain under the cerebrum. The black antlike nerve cells are named *Purkinje cells* after their discoverer, Jan Evangelista Purkinje, a Czech doctor. They have countless numbers of dendrites—someone once figured that the human body has hundreds of thousands of miles of them. Since dendrites receive information, you know that the cerebellum processes an enormous amount of information.

It is the job of the cerebellum to coordinate your skeletal movement. The cerebrum says it wants you to dance or throw a ball and the cerebellum coordinates all the nerves that tell the right muscles to contract. When you get really good at an activity, it is because the cerebellum is programmed to make the right moves. A concert pianist does not have to consciously tell each finger where to go. Hours of practice have programmed the cerebellum.

Drinking alcohol affects the cerebellum. That's why too much alcohol makes people lose their coordination and prevents them from walking a straight line.

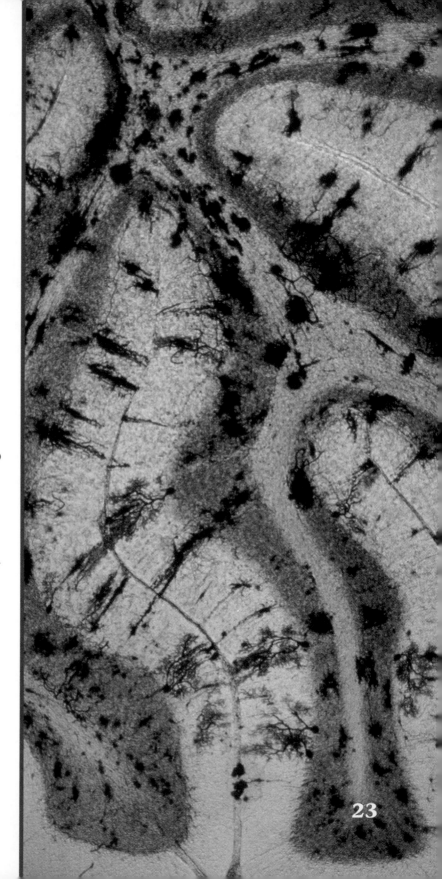

23

Digestion

You grow. You move. You heal. You interact with the world. All of this takes energy and building materials. The source is food. So what, exactly, is food? Actually, it is other once-living things. The animals and plants we eat are made up of carbohydrates, proteins, and fats—large, complicated molecules found in all living things. The trouble is that these food molecules are different from our molecules. But interestingly, all carbohydrates, proteins, and fats, no matter where they come from, are built from smaller molecules—much as words are made from an alphabet. Foods have the same alphabet we have but they are in different languages. You can think of broken-down food molecules as the letters of the alphabet that we use to write our own words.

It is the job of digestion to break down carbohydrates into simple sugars, proteins into amino acids, and fats into fatty acids. The smaller molecules are then absorbed into the blood and transported around the body. The sugars are used for energy, the amino acids are used to build your own proteins, and the fatty acids have a variety of jobs. The scanning electron microscope takes a closer look at some of the structures in your digestive tract.

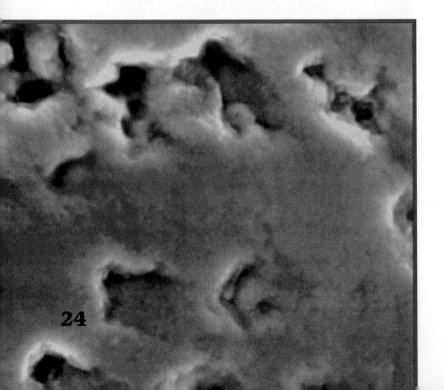

Tougher Than Nails

The outer covering of your teeth—the **enamel**— is the hardest substance in your body. This SEM shows the enamel surface of a tooth. Its hardness comes from calcium and phosphate minerals. The mineral crystals are densely packed in the shape of rods that run from the inside of the tooth to its surface. You can see the circular pattern of the ends of the rods in this SEM.

Enamel minerals are the same minerals that make your bones hard. Milk is the source of minerals for teeth and bones. It's especially important to drink milk when you're a kid.

24

But bone minerals are not as densely packed and contain spaces where there are living bone cells. Enamel is almost completely mineral and the cells that formed it are no longer alive. The body can't repair damaged tooth enamel.

Teeth need to be hard. Their job is to begin the process of digestion by mechanically grinding up food so that the digestive juices can start working on it. Tooth enamel can withstand a lifetime—eighty years or more— of cutting and grinding.

Lickin' Good

If you scrape the edge of your fingernail on your tongue, you can feel its roughness. This SEM shows the many *papillae*—or tiny projections— that cover most of the surface of your tongue and give it its texture. The smaller and more numerous papillae are colored blue. They are called *filiform* (or "threadlike") *papillae* because sometimes there are long protein threads attached to the ends like pennants on a flagpole. Filiform papillae sense temperature and the irritating chemicals that make spicy dishes hot.

The larger, flat, circular papillae are called *fungiform papillae* because they are shaped like mushrooms, with a larger head on a slender neck. There are between two hundred and four hundred fungiform papillae on the tongue and they contain all of the taste buds—the sense organs for sweet, sour, salty, and bitter. Up to twenty taste buds are located under the surface of a fungiform papillae and connect to the surface through tiny pores. These papillae make sure we enjoy our food so that we continue to eat throughout our life.

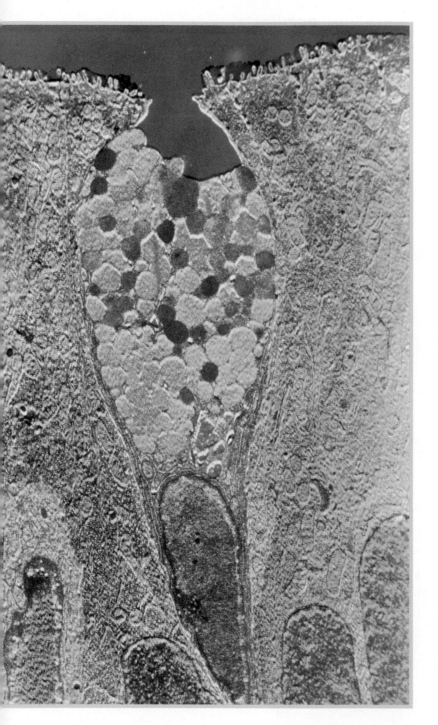

Gobs of Goo

As food slides through the digestive tract, mucus makes sure it stays slippery. Otherwise, traveling food could be very irritating. This SEM shows a cell in the act of manufacturing mucus. It's called a **goblet cell.** The tiny blue circles are drops of mucus. This goblet cell opens into the beginning of the small intestine. It is surrounded by cells with tiny fingerlike projections, called **villi,** that form a carpet at the surface. Villi absorb the important nutritional parts of food as it moves past. The carrot-shaped object at the bottom of the goblet cell is its nucleus. The mucus is manufactured by the purple network surrounding the nucleus.

Guts

By the time food has passed through your stomach to your guts, or *small intestine*, it is completely liquid and ready to be absorbed into your body. Absorption is the job of the small intestine. The SEM below shows the villi on the inner surface of the first part of the small intestine. Villi increase the surface area of the intestine to the size of an average room in your home. Each villus is lined with capillaries.

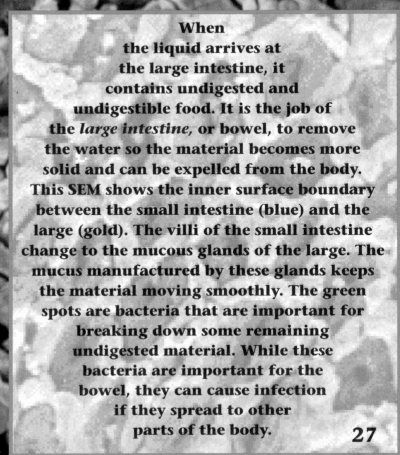

When the liquid arrives at the large intestine, it contains undigested and undigestible food. It is the job of the *large intestine,* or bowel, to remove the water so the material becomes more solid and can be expelled from the body. This SEM shows the inner surface boundary between the small intestine (blue) and the large (gold). The villi of the small intestine change to the mucous glands of the large. The mucus manufactured by these glands keeps the material moving smoothly. The green spots are bacteria that are important for breaking down some remaining undigested material. While these bacteria are important for the bowel, they can cause infection if they spread to other parts of the body.

27

Respiration

● ● ● ● ● ● ●

Take a deep breath. Your lungs are now filled with air. About one-fifth of the air is the life-giving gas called oxygen. Why is it life-giving? For the same reason fire burns. When oxygen combines with fuel, energy is released. A fire is the heat and light energy. If you burned food like a fire, you wouldn't be alive. But your body has ways of combining food (a fuel) with oxygen slowly, step by step. In this way, the energy is released in a controlled way so that it can be used for movement, thinking, feeling, growing, healing, and every other living activity.

Fire produces waste products—carbon dioxide and water. So does your body. The process by which you take in oxygen gas and give off carbon dioxide gas is called *respiration.* The scene of the action is the lungs.

An Airy Place

Your lungs are basically two expandable spongy bags with lots of pockets for air to go. The air tube, or *bronchus,* that enters each lung, branches like a tree. It becomes smaller and smaller, dividing into about thirty thousand little branches, or *bronchioles.* The walls of the bronchioles contain tiny round openings called *alveoli.* A full-grown person has about three hundred million alveoli, which create a surface of about fifty times larger than the skin, or about one hundred square yards. The gas exchange—taking in oxygen and giving off carbon dioxide—takes place in the alveoli. Tiny capillaries deliver blood to the alveoli.

This colored SEM of the lung shows the alveoli in yellow, an air passageway in blue, and a large blood vessel in red. This low magnification doesn't show the capillaries in the alveoli.

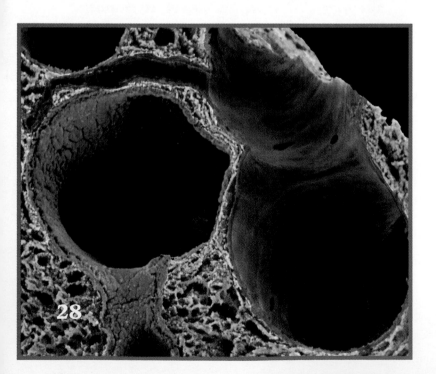

28

But this one does. At more than four million times its actual size, you can see three red cells squashed in a capillary in the act of exchanging gases. Notice how very thin the capillary wall is. The red cells get extremely close to the alveoli. The walls of the capillary and the red cell membranes are so thin that gas molecules can easily pass through them. From the lungs, the oxygen-rich blood returns to the heart, which then sends it on its way to the rest of the body.

Attention:
This Is a No-Smoking Message

**This is a low-magnification slide
of a normal lung taken through
a light microscope. You can't see
too much detail except for the pink
color and the dense cell structure.**

A smoker's lung at the same magnification looks very different. The alveoli walls are broken, like torn cobwebs. Black tars are deposited throughout the delicate tissues. Smoking causes a disease called *emphysema*. A person with emphysema has a very hard time getting enough oxygen. That's because the alveoli walls are broken and the lungs have lost a lot of their ability to contract. As a result, they contain too much air that they can't expel. A person with emphysema suffers even more when he or she has to move faster. Normal lungs have no problem increasing oxygen intake when there is increased activity.

In addition to emphysema, smoking has been shown to cause almost one in every three deaths by cancer and it is a major cause of heart disease. It is very difficult to quit once you start. About half of all the adults in the United States who started smoking when they were young have quit smoking. But it took most of them three or four tries before they were successful.

Even if you don't smoke, hanging around people who do can be harmful to your health. Smoke that comes off a burning cigarette tip has more cancer-causing chemicals than smoke inhaled directly. That's why so many states have passed laws banning smoking in public places.

You have heard a lot about never smoking—these pictures show you the damage smoking causes.

Making the Pictures

The ordinary light microscope can show us only structures that are thin enough to let light pass through them. So you are usually looking at a slice of something at most fourteen hundred times its actual size. The scanning electron microscope, lets us see the surfaces of structures in three dimensions rather than a slice through them. It is also capable of enormous magnification. The most highly magnified picture in this book is the SEM of red blood cells (page 4 left), which is magnified more than nine million times.

The scanning electron microscope doesn't look anything like an ordinary microscope. For one thing, it's a lot larger. For another, it has a lot more parts to it. This is a picture of Dennis Kunkel, a University of Hawaii microscopist, sitting at his scanning electron microscope, which he has affectionately named "Zoom." The picture he sees of the specimen is on the TV screen on the panel in front of him. The television picture is created by a tiny beam of electrons—negatively charged particles—that scans back and forth in lines across the TV screen. The scanning is so fast, at sixty times a second, that you see it as if the entire screen is lit up all at once. A similar type of scanning is used in the electron microscope.

The top of the long column on Dennis's left contains an electron gun, which shoots a stream of electrons at a specimen below it. The specimen is coated with a thin layer of gold before it is placed in the specimen chamber below the gun. The entire insides of the microscope are connected to a vacuum pump because air interferes with the path of the electrons. When the electron beam is scanned over the specimen, it excites the gold molecules to release their electrons. These excited electrons are collected and sent to the TV viewing screen. The pattern of the electrons shows up as light and shadow on the screen. The black-and-white picture looks like a bird's-eye view of the specimen's surface.

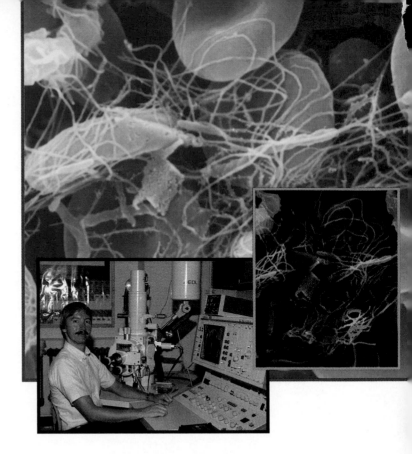

When he finds an image he likes on the screen, Dennis can take a photograph called a micrograph. The scanning electron microscope can produce only a black-and-white image like the large micrograph. It is colored later by hand or by computer. The artists who do the coloring must know what they are looking at in order to color the black-and-white image.

Index